COVENANT RELATIONSHIPS

a Lifetime of Fulfilment

GORDON TOSE

COVENANT RELATIONSHIPS (a Lifetime of Fulfilment)
Gordon Tose
Huddersfield Christian Fellowship
Copyright © 2011 Cathedral House Media
The author asserts the moral right to be identified as the author of this work in accordance with
the Copyright, Design and Patents Act 1988

Cover Design and Layout by Marcus Woolcock

Published & Distributed by:

 CATHEDRAL HOUSE
MEDIA

Cathedral House
St Thomas Road
Huddersfield
HD1 3LG
www.huddersfieldchristianfellowship.com

ISBN 978-0-9569079-0-5

First Edition 2011
All rights reserved

ACKNOWLEDGEMENTS

This booklet would not have been possible without the input of the following people: My Pastor, Colin Cooper, who asked me to write it in the first place and then gave me the opportunity to do so; my wife, Marjorie, whose constant encouragement has always been a positive influence in my life; and my two covenant friends whose continuing commitment towards me has demonstrated the practical outworking of this biblical principle. Many thanks to them all.

I would also like to thank Marcus Woolcock, not only for his expertise in producing the 'end result', but also for his patience in putting up with my lack of expertise.

Contents

The Church's Need of Relationships   7

The Challenge of Relationships   11

Covenant Relationships   17

The Making of Covenant   25

The Ingredients of Covenant   29

The Consequences of Covenant   35

The Benefit of Covenant   41

The Church's Need of Relationships

I love the Local Church, my Local Church that is; Huddersfield Christian Fellowship. I love it, I really do. In fact I would go further and say that I love the whole concept of the Local Church; probably because my experience of it has been so positive. My family and I first attended the Fellowship back in February 1988, (twenty three years ago at the time of writing this booklet) and over the years I have grown to value it and appreciate its importance. The Bible refers to the Church as the 'Family of God' and that is how I view my Church; it is my extended family. As for its importance, I would say that the Local Church is the main vehicle, or it should be, by which the Kingdom of God is established and extended; that is its purpose. Unfortunately, many churches seem to be unsuccessful in fulfilling this purpose and the reason for this would appear to be a lack of strong relationships between the members. In other words, they may be the 'Family of God' by name, but not by nature. **It has been my experience that only relationships keep people together.**

Let me tell you what does not keep people together:-

Shared Doctrine:

You can have a group of people who all believe more or less the same things. They may all passionately believe in the deity of Jesus Christ, in His crucifixion and His resurrection and they may all look forward to His second coming. They may all be baptised in water and be in full agreement with the baptism of the Holy Spirit and the manifestation of the Gifts of the Spirit. However, it would appear that this sharing of beliefs is not sufficient in itself to keep people from leaving Church, and all they do, when they leave for whatever reason, is find another group whose beliefs match their own. Of course they could not do that in New Testament times because if they left the Church in Corinth, maybe if they had fallen out with someone or their own ambitions were not being met, there was nowhere else for them to go, whereas these days people are spoilt for choice.

A Great Church Programme:

You can have the most imaginative programme it is possible to have. There can be something for everybody, a youth programme and a Sunday school programme that is inspirational, the needs of every section of the congregation well and truly met. You can be well organised, have the right balance between social and spiritual activities and there can be plenty of opportunity for people to exercise their gifts; yet people will still leave the Church and find somewhere else to worship.

Excellent Facilities:

Huddersfield Christian Fellowship is blessed with great facilities. We moved into our new premises, Cathedral House, towards the end of 2008 and, without exaggerating, it would be fair to say that the new building has caused quite a stir both locally and nationally (and even internationally). However, even our previous building was special enough for two television companies each to do a live broadcast from it. But the point I am trying to make is that great facilities will not ensure that people remain together, and over the years I have seen many people leave this Church and go to other churches that, by comparison, have vastly inferior facilities.

Anointed Ministry:

The thing about anointing is that people can get used to it, they can become familiar with it. This was brought home to me when I accompanied my Pastor to a Church in Finland a few years ago. During the Sunday morning service he was preaching a sermon I had heard numerous times before and my thoughts began to wander. I realise we should never tire of hearing God's Word, but certainly on that particular occasion my mind was elsewhere. I am not even sure I was aware that he had come to the end of his message and was making his appeal. However, my attention was re-engaged when just about the whole Church responded to the appeal and it became obvious that the Holy Spirit was ministering to God's people. That particular episode taught me a valuable lesson that there is indeed truth to the saying that 'familiarity breeds contempt'. It is this over-familiarity with ministry, even anointed ministry, that convinces some people that there is truth in another saying that 'the grass is always greener on the other side'.

The Presence of God:

I still find it staggering that even the presence of God will not keep people together and we see this even in the ministry of Jesus. When Jesus performed His miracles - when the blind were able to see, the deaf hear, the lame walk and when evil spirits were cast out - He drew a huge crowd. They were attracted to the 'happenings'. Yet as soon as He began to teach the things of the Kingdom, most of the crowd left Him.

John 6:60 & 66

On hearing it, many of his disciples said, "This is a hard teaching. Who can accept it?"......From this time many of his disciples turned back and no longer followed him.

Of course the Local Church should possess all these ingredients. It needs an imaginative programme that enables its people to actively participate. It needs its people to more or less be in one accord with their beliefs. Good facilities are not essential but they are helpful. And without a measure of anointing and the presence of God there is not much point in gathering together in the first place. However, it appears that none of these ingredients stop people leaving, and stopping people leaving is important for a number of reasons, not least of which is that the fewer the number of people who leave, the bigger each Local Church becomes and with greater size comes greater influence.

> ## What every Church needs to understand is that the extent of its effectiveness will depend on the strength of the relationships within it.

I am a great believer in big churches (relative to the size of the local community) because every Church should aspire to be influential within its locality and this can only be achieved if people know that the Church is there. It is true that big is not always beautiful but it is generally influential. For example - if the President of a country of little international significance made an announcement about something, probably not too many people worldwide would take much notice. However, if the President of the USA made a similar announcement, the chances are that the whole world would take note. The size of the Church is therefore important, which makes discouraging people from leaving absolutely vital, because what every Church needs to understand is that **the extent of its effectiveness will depend on the strength of the relationships within it.**

The Challenge of Relationships

The subject of 'relationships' is actually very easy to teach, the biblical principles being easily understandable, but these same principles can be very difficult to live in, day in day out, year in year out. The reason for this is that maintaining good relationships with each other, close relationships, certainly over the long term, is something that does not come naturally to us and we see this highlighted in Jesus' prayer in the Garden of Gethsemane.

John 17:20 & 23
"My prayer is not for them alone. I pray also for those who will believe in me through their message......May they be brought to complete unity to let the world know that you sent me and have loved them even as you have loved me."

So here we have Jesus facing crucifixion. He has already prayed for Himself, He has then prayed for His disciples, *"My prayer is not for them alone,"* and He now prays *"for those who will believe in me."* In other words He prays for all who, since the time of Jesus, have subsequently accepted Him as their Lord and

Saviour. Crucifixion was not something that Jesus was looking forward to and in fact the prospect of it put Him under tremendous emotional distress.

Matthew 26:38
Then he said to them, (talking to His disciples) *"My soul is overwhelmed with sorrow to the point of death."*

Luke 22:44
And being in anguish, he prayed more earnestly, and his sweat was like drops of blood falling to the ground.

Sweating blood is an actual physical phenomenon known as 'hematohidrosis', that can occur when we are so emotionally stressed that the blood capillaries around the sweat glands burst, and as we sweat, we do literally sweat blood. Yet despite what He was going through, the thing uppermost in His mind was our relationships; *"May they be brought to complete unity."* That is truly amazing.

This prayer of Jesus was, in a way, His last chance to really connect with His Father before He went to His death. The words we speak in this kind of situation, when we face the inevitability of death, are obviously of great importance to us. King David on his death bed shares his heart with his son Solomon:

1 Kings 2:2-4
"I am about to go the way of all the earth," he said. "So be strong, show yourself a man, and observe what the LORD your God requires: Walk in his ways, and keep his decrees and commands, his laws and requirements, as written in the Law of Moses, so that you may prosper in all you do and wherever you go, and that the LORD may keep his promise to me: 'If your descendants watch how they live, and if they walk faithfully before me with all their heart and soul, you will never fail to have a man on the throne of Israel.'"

When the Apostle Paul was in prison waiting to be executed, his last letter to Timothy, his spiritual son, was again a final sharing of his heart, a communication of those things that he considered to be of the utmost importance; things such as relationships, persecution and Timothy's ministry. So going back to Jesus, the first thing we have to understand, especially considering the circumstances, is that **our relationships are of the utmost importance to God.**

> ## Although 'Covenant' is only one aspect of relationships, it can nevertheless guarantee that certain relationships last for a lifetime.

The second thing we have to understand is that keeping our relationships as they should be is hard work.

Ephesians 4:1-3
*As a prisoner for the Lord, then, **I urge you** to live a life worthy of the calling you have received. Be completely humble and gentle; be patient, **bearing with one another** in love. **Make every effort** to keep the unity of the Spirit through the bond of peace.*

It always makes me smile when I think of who actually wrote that scripture. Obviously it was Paul and yet Paul himself was prone to 'falling out' with people. In fact his disagreement with Barnabas in Acts 15 was such that he split their ministry. He also argued with Peter and while he may have been correct in what he said, what is undoubtedly true is that his rebuke of Peter was overly aggressive.

Galatians 2:11 & 14
*When Peter came to Antioch, I opposed him to his face, because he was clearly in the wrong...... I said to Peter **in front of them all**, "You are a Jew, yet you live like a Gentile and not like a Jew. How is it, then, that you force Gentiles to follow Jewish customs?"*

Even the disciples, who had sat at the feet of Jesus and experienced first hand His teaching on loving each other, argued among themselves. Of course the lesson we can learn from this is that if the great Apostle Paul experienced difficulties in maintaining relational harmony, as did the disciples, then we too will experience the same difficulties. But why should that be? Why is it so difficult for us to maintain right relationships? Well, as I said earlier, it appears to be something that does not come naturally to us, and while this may sound a bit pessimistic, it would explain why Jesus felt He had to pray for us, *"May they be brought to complete unity* **to let the world know that you sent me and have loved them even as you have loved me."** In fact what Jesus is saying here is that relational unity, or relational harmony, is so unnatural to us that when it exists it points to the reality of God.

However, if maintaining good relationships is so difficult, what is the motivation for us to put in the hard work, other than of course the knowledge that this is what Jesus wants from us? Our motivation, and this is the third principle we need to understand, comes from an appreciation that where good relationships exist so also does God's blessing.

Psalm 133:1-3
How good and pleasant it is when brothers live together in unity! (When sisters live together in unity/when the Church lives together in unity) *It is like precious oil poured on the head, running down on the beard, running down on Aaron's beard, down upon the collar of his robes. It is as if the dew of Hermon were falling on Mount Zion. For there the LORD bestows his blessing, even life for evermore.*

In the King James Version, instead of the word *bestows* in verse 3, it uses the word *commanded. For there the LORD commanded the blessing.* It is like a law, an inescapable law, a bit like gravity. Gravity is a natural law which we are all subject to. It does not matter how high we try to jump, or how much effort we put into the jump, we leave the ground, but not for long; we cannot escape the effects of gravity. But as there are natural laws, so there are also spiritual laws that we are equally subject to. 'Sowing and reaping' is one such law: Galatians 6: 7 *Do not be deceived: God cannot be mocked. A man reaps what he sows.* If we sow good things in our life then we will reap good things, but the opposite is also true even to the extent that we will still reap a bad harvest as a Christian because of the bad things we sowed as a non-Christian. Another such law, equally inescapable, is that **relational unity releases the blessing of God.** It seems to be a reward by God for our willingness to put in the hard work. This is why the subject of 'covenant relationships' is so important. Although it is only one aspect of relationships, it is an aspect that, if understood, can guarantee that certain relationships last even for a lifetime. This, in turn, releases God's blessing on both the Church corporately and on us as individuals.

Covenant Relationships

I want to begin by considering the act of marriage which is the obvious expression of a covenant relationship. When two people marry, they generally do not do so the very first time they meet. I am obviously not referring to an arranged marriage, although even with arranged marriages the couple is normally allowed a period of time to get to know each other. I feel confident in saying therefore, that marriage is something that is entered into by two people who are already in relationship with each other. In other words, their existing relationship has reached a particular stage where the two individuals want to commit themselves to each other. In our society it seems that more and more couples, instead of marrying, prefer as an alternative, to simply live together. They would argue that living together is really the same as marriage, the only difference being the lack of a certificate. However, the contention that the marriage certificate is only a 'piece of paper' is nothing more than a strategy, realised or not, designed to avoid making any serious statement of commitment. Of course, whatever the prevailing culture, married life tends to start with some form of ceremony, in other words, some kind of event that marks the beginning of this new stage in the relationship. Obviously the content of the ceremony will differ depending on the culture, but nevertheless I feel I can make the assumption that most ceremonies will include an element of the making of promises and the exchanging of tokens. Then as we all know, certainly those of us who are married, this commitment one to another, should involve elements such as faithfulness and sacrifice. The reason I am focussing on marriage this way is because I am of the firm conviction that **God wants us to have relationships with each other governed by the same principles as marriage.**

When looking at the subject of covenant relationships, the obvious biblical example is the relationship that existed between David and Jonathan with the pertinent scripture being 1 Samuel 18:1-4:

> *After David had finished talking with Saul, Jonathan became one in spirit with David, and he loved him as himself. From that day Saul kept David with him and did not let him return to his father's house. And Jonathan made a covenant with David because he loved him as himself. Jonathan took off the robe he was wearing and gave it to David, along with his tunic, and even his sword, his bow and his belt.*

What I am suggesting is that David and Jonathan already had a relationship. The way I have often heard this particular scripture presented is that Jonathan walks into the room where he sees David for the first time. He has more than likely heard of David, as the killing of Goliath would have been the hot topic of the day. Their eyes meet, there is a Holy Spirit connection and they make a covenant there and then! While I do not want to presume to dismiss this interpretation of events out of hand, what I would say is that the events detailed in the Bible are there for us to relate to and learn from:

2 Timothy 3: 16-17
All scripture is God breathed and is useful for teaching, rebuking, correcting and training in righteousness, so that the man of God

(and the woman of God) *may be thoroughly equipped for every good work.*

Yes there had been a connection between the two of them but that connection had led to the beginning of a relationship which grew, albeit quickly, to the point where they wanted to do something that would somehow **guarantee that their relationship lasted.**

God wants us to have relationships with each other governed by the same principles as marriage.

Some time ago I heard someone preaching on this subject. During the message the preacher listed all the people he had a covenant relationship with, and there were quite a number, and the impression I got was that his evidence of the existence of a covenant was the length of time he had been in these relationships. However, longevity of relationship is not evidence of covenant. That is like comparing couples who choose to live together with couples who are married. Marriage is a covenant, living together is not. The preacher also gave the impression that covenant was evidenced by the intimacy of his relationships. But no matter how intimate a relationship is, intimacy in itself will not guarantee that a relationship will last. Sadly, most of us can look back over our lives and recall people we were once close to, in some cases very close, but who now are no longer part of our lives. Covenant, and not intimacy, is the means by which relationships last.

What we can also see from David and Jonathan's covenant is that *Jonathan **made** a covenant with David.* The covenant was not assumed. To assume the existence of a covenant based on longevity and/or intimacy is just that; it is an assumption. **Covenant should never be assumed.** We do not assume we are married, hence the reason for the ceremony which includes the making of the covenant. The ceremony is something we can look back on and see when the covenant began. In David and Jonathan's case we see that *Jonathan took off the robe he was wearing and gave it to David, along with his tunic and even his sword, his bow and his belt.* These were the tokens of the covenant made, very much like the wedding ring which is to remind us of the covenant we have entered into. It may well be that David had none of these items and that they would most certainly prove useful, even essential, and yet Jonathan was not acting out the role of supplies officer. He was giving David certain items which, when David wore them and used them, would be visible evidence of their covenant.

Carrying on the comparison between covenant relationships generally and marriage in particular, we see in 1 Samuel 20:12-17 the ingredients of sacrifice, faithfulness and reaffirmation.

> *Then Jonathan said to David: "By the LORD, the God of Israel, I will surely sound out my father by this time the day after tomorrow! If he is favourably disposed towards you, will I not send you word and let you know? But if my father is inclined to harm you, may the LORD deal with me, be it ever so severely, if I do not let you know and send you away safely. May the LORD be with you as he has been with my father. But show me unfailing kindness like that of the LORD as long as I live, so that I may not be killed, and do not ever cut off your kindness from my family – not even when the LORD has cut off every one of David's enemies from the face of the earth." So Jonathan made a covenant with the house of David, saying, "May the LORD call David's enemies to account." And Jonathan made David reaffirm his oath out of love for him, because he loved him as he loved himself.*

Their covenant involved sacrifice in that when Jonathan came to the decision to take sides with David against his father Saul, he effectively relinquished his right to be the heir to the throne of Israel. In effect, his covenant with David cost Jonathan his birthright.

It also involved faithfulness in that David, having promised Jonathan that he would take care of his family in the event of Jonathan's death, takes in Jonathan's son Mephibosheth and treats him as if he was his own flesh and blood.

2 Samuel 9:3-7
The king (David) *asked, "Is there no-one still left of the house of Saul to whom I can show God's kindness?"* Ziba (who had been a servant of Saul) *answered the king, "There is still a son of Jonathan; he is crippled in both feet."......When Mephibosheth son of Jonathan, the son of Saul, came to David, he bowed down to pay him honour. ...... "Don't be afraid," David said to him, "for I will surely show you kindness for the sake of your father Jonathan. I will restore to you all the land that belonged to your grandfather Saul, and you will always eat at my table."*

This act of faithfulness was all the more impressive for two reasons. Firstly, as Jonathan was dead, David could easily have gone back on his promise knowing full well that no one would take him to task. Secondly, the accepted custom of those times was that any new king would systematically arrange the death of any surviving male relatives of the previous king in order to prevent a counter coup. Admittedly Mephibosheth would probably pose little threat, if any, to David's position, but nobody would have criticised him if he had arranged for Mephibosheth to be put to death.

Finally, as with any close relationship, there was the need for reaffirmation: *And Jonathan made David* **reaffirm** *his oath out of love for him.* It has often been the case that one party of a relationship will assume that the other party knows that the relationship is as solid as it has always been. Certainly there is truth in the saying that 'actions speak louder than words', but we should never underestimate the value of words, and in any relationship it is vital that we verbally communicate our continuing commitment to it.

It is important we understand that we were created by God as relational beings and it is my contention that our capacity for relationship exceeds what we get from being married. Let me try to explain what I mean by that, although obviously I am speaking from a male perspective (although I suspect it is no different from a female perspective). As a man I need someone who truly understands what it is to be a man. A woman does not understand, not fully; she is not a man so how could she? A man does not understand what it is to be a woman. I have been married for over thirty years and even though I know my wife intimately, and in fact she is without doubt my best friend, nevertheless she will occasionally do things, or more often than not she will react to things in a way that completely catches me by surprise. I am not saying that life is not worth living if we do not have these other kind of relationships. I could quite happily live my life with my only meaningful relationships being those with my wife and two sons, but what these other relationships do is enrich our lives. As a man I need someone, other than my wife, with whom I can laugh, and indeed I relate with a number of men on that kind of level. However, if that is the depth of the relationship then it may well be fun but it is also superficial, and my need for relationship goes beyond that. Finding someone, other than my wife, with whom I can share my thoughts and my heart is much more difficult. To share your heart with someone is to make yourself vulnerable and that is risky which is why we do not have many relationships of that depth. I heard a preacher say that "vulnerability is offering an opening to be criticised" and as a general principle nobody likes to be criticised. But I would go further and say that as a man I need someone, other men, who I can cry with, and while that kind of relationship is rare because it entails exposing yourself emotionally, where that depth of relationship exists, there is true relational fulfilment.

David and Jonathan had that depth of relationship. After Jonathan's death at the hands of the Philistines, David wrote in 2 Samuel 1:26:

> *I grieve for you, Jonathan my brother; you were very dear to me. Your love for me was wonderful, more wonderful than that of women.*

> *Oh my dear brother Jonathan, I'm crushed by your death. Your friendship was a miracle-wonder, love far exceeding anything I've known - or ever hope to know.* (The Message)

Jonathan, I miss you most! I loved you like a brother. You were truly loyal to me, more faithful than a wife to her husband. (Contemporary English Version)

One commentator wrote of that verse: "David is not suggesting that marital love is inferior to friendship, nor do his remarks have any sexual implications. He is simply calling attention to Jonathan's nearly inexplicable self-denying commitment to David."

Therefore, what I am suggesting is that where a relationship exists, and there is a desire by both parties that the relationship should last 'until death do us part', then the way to guarantee that is to make a covenant.

The Making of Covenant

Covenant must never be assumed, covenant has to be made. What must also be realised is that the making of covenant is a serious business because **when we make a covenant, we make it before God.** The seriousness of covenant making is seen in the covenant that God made with Abram.

> **Genesis 15:9-18**
> *So the LORD said to him, "Bring me a heifer, a goat and a ram, each three years old, along with a dove and a young pigeon." Abram brought all these to him, cut them in two and arranged the halves opposite each other...... As the sun was setting, Abram fell into a deep sleep, and a thick and dreadful darkness came over him...... When the sun had set and darkness had fallen, a smoking brazier with a blazing torch appeared and passed between the pieces. On that day the LORD made a covenant with Abram.*

What this scripture is emphasising, and it is vital that this principle is understood, is that if covenant is subsequently broken, then the blood that was spilled when the covenant was made would be on the hands of the covenant breaker.

Covenant, like marriage, is supposed to last a lifetime, and yet over the years I have known people make a covenant, and some of these people have been Church leaders of some maturity and indeed seniority, but then for a variety of reasons the relationship they had with each other either stops abruptly or just fades away. It appears that what was entered into was, in effect, a conditional covenant. Maybe the covenant was conditional on one of the parties continuing to benefit from the relationship, and when the benefit ceased, so too did the relationship. Maybe it was conditional on the continuing presence of one of the parties; in other words, the covenant was only intended to last while their paths continued to cross. Maybe it was conditional on there being no reason to be offended with each other, and when offence came the relationship was not strong enough to overcome it. However, there are no 'get out' clauses in a covenant. On the contrary, covenant is a lifelong commitment, which is why we should never enter into one with someone we do not really know.

The making of covenant is a serious business because it is made before God.

But how do we go about actually making a covenant? The answer is quite simple in that there is no prescribed method, the only criteria being that it has to be literally made. There has to be an event that can be looked back on that marks its beginning. When I first came across the principle of covenant I really wanted to make it work because I recognised my desire to have some long-term, meaningful relationships in my life. My only concern was how to go about it. I already had a friendship with two men both of whom I really felt connected to. I also thought I understood the gravity of what I wanted to do. But what about 'the event'? What would be the best way to approach them both? Would they understand what I was trying to do? How would they respond?

Because of the relationship I had with one of them, I decided to write him a letter. In this letter I wrote that I **would** let him down (note the use of the word "would" and not "might") but that it would never be intentional. I also wrote that **when** he let me down (not "if" he let me down but "when") that I would never walk away from him. Over the years it would be fair to say that we have indeed let each other down, maybe in ways that under normal circumstances would have resulted in a breakdown of the relationship. It would also be fair to say that our relationship has continued to evolve, much as you would expect a marriage relationship to evolve. This is due to the experiences we have shared and the fact that it has become a long-term relationship which has led to a greater understanding of each other. However, the point is that the relationship has been maintained, and one reason for this is because of the existence of a covenant, made before God, the evidence of which is a letter. What I am not suggesting is that we all go around writing letters to each other. This was just my attempt at making a covenant, and at the time it seemed to me to be the best way to establish it.

The personality of my other friend was very different to that of the recipient of my letter. I really was not sure he would understand what I was trying to do, but I was again mindful of the need for there to be some kind of starting point to this new stage in the relationship. So as a token of the covenant I gave him a used toothbrush!!! Please, please bear with me. Why something as ridiculous as a used toothbrush? Do not forget that the whole concept of covenant was new to me and my thinking was that if he did not understand what I was trying to achieve then I could pass it all off as a joke and hopefully retain some of my dignity. Some years later I was in a Church in Kenya teaching on this very subject and wanting to use the toothbrush example. In order to maintain some preaching integrity I thought it was right to check if he still had it. So as I was waiting to preach, I sent him a quick text message which he did not respond to but to which his wife did. In her reply she said that of course he still had it because it was something of value to him. In other words my old toothbrush is tangible evidence that he has at least one friend who he can rely on come what may. When my wife looks down and sees the wedding ring on her finger, that ring is evidence to her that she has somebody who will defend her even when she is in the wrong, somebody who will love her during those times when she is not very loveable, and someone who will be by her side until one of us dies. And it is the same with my covenant brothers.

The Ingredients of Covenant

For covenant relationships to be maintained they have to have certain ingredients. One such ingredient is **LOYALTY.** The problem in assessing loyalty is that we do not know how loyal we are until our loyalty is tested. Another problem in assessing loyalty is that everybody assumes it is a characteristic they possess. I have lost count over the years of the times that I have asked congregations the question: "How many disloyal and unfaithful people do we have in Church today?" As you would expect, I have not been met with an overwhelming response and yet this is what the Bible says in Proverbs 20:6:

> *Many a man claims to have unfailing love, but a faithful man who can find?*
>
> *Everyone talks about how loyal and faithful he is, but just try to find someone who really is!* (Good News Version)

What makes loyalty so difficult to maintain is that it is only called for in the face of relational upset; when we have been hurt by a friend, or let down by them. Maybe they have offended us in some way; probably unintentionally but not necessarily so. Maybe they have acted in a way that while it did not adversely affect us, it was nevertheless an action that we disagreed with. However, none of these situations, in general terms, is an acceptable reason to break up a relationship.

The reality is that nobody is perfect and we all accept that. In fact we would think it totally unreasonable if anybody expected anything like perfection from us, and yet when someone else displays their imperfection to us, so often our response is: "How dare they!"

1 Peter 4:8
Above all, love each other deeply, because love covers over a multitude of sins.

That scripture is not telling us to ignore the sin in the lives of others, or worse still to condone it. But what it is saying to us is that we should make provision for someone else's failure. We should make allowances for their imperfection as we would hope that they would make allowances for our imperfection. Loyalty is a decision not to "*look at the speck of sawdust in your brother's eye*" and instead to "*pay attention to the plank in your own eye.*"

1 Corinthians 13:5
it (love) *keeps no record of wrongs.*

I recognised the truth of this scripture when I realised that I could not remember what it was that one of my covenant brothers had done to me that hurt me so much a number of years earlier. It was not that the whole incident had been erased from my memory as if it had never occurred, but what had happened was that my love for my friend had enabled me not to dwell on the incident to such an extent that the details no longer had any hold over me.

Why should our friendships fail because of a display of imperfection when our marriages do not? The answer to that, at least in part, is that our marriage relationship has been formalised which helps keep it together. If we formalised our friendships, would that not have the same effect?

Of course we may experience such severe difficulties in the relationship that it inevitably disintegrates, and while this is unfortunate in the extreme, it is what happens even in marriage, even in Christian marriages. However, what we must be ever mindful of is another necessary ingredient and that is a **WILLINGNESS TO FORGIVE**. In 'The Parable of the Unmerciful Servant' in Matthew 18:21-22 Peter asks Jesus: *"Lord, how many times shall I forgive my brother when he sins against me? Up to seven times?" Jesus answered, "I tell you, not seven times, but seventy-seven times."* Jesus' response is meant to demonstrate that our forgiveness of someone is not to be limited to a certain number of times.

Also our forgiveness is to be given irrespective of how we feel. It is certainly true that forgiveness is motivated by love, but when Jesus tells us to *"Love your neighbour as yourself"* in Matthew 22:39, the kind of love He is referring to is the Greek word 'agapē'; in other words a love that is not based on feelings but is an act of the will. How this works out is that we may not feel like forgiving someone. We may not want to continue with the relationship. However, we are still called to forgive, and to do so willingly. Therefore, forgiveness must be from the heart whether we feel like it or not.

Matthew 18:35
"This is how my heavenly Father will treat each of you unless you forgive your brother from your heart."

In 1 Samuel 16:7 we are told that *"Man looks at the outward appearance, but the LORD looks at the heart."* In other words, God sees what is behind our words and He sees what is behind our actions. *'The Greatest Commandment'* as defined by Jesus in Matthew 22:37 is to *"Love the Lord your God with all your heart and with all your soul and with all your mind."* Notice that it is the heart that comes first and that is because when we talk of our heart we talk of how we really feel, and **saying** we forgive is not necessarily the same as forgiving. Therefore, forgiveness is not just a matter of words; it is a matter of feelings. Or to be more accurate, it is a matter of overcoming our feelings.

Forgiveness is also a matter of self-protection in that when we choose not to forgive, and it is a choice, we choose to inflict pain on ourselves. There are numerous examples throughout the Bible of what I would call 'sad verses'. For example, Judges 16:20 where it says of Samson: *But he did not know that the LORD had left him.* Another such verse is Proverbs 14:13 which says: *Even in laughter the heart may ache.* And when unforgiveness persists to the detriment of a relationship, then the negative feelings we experience always seem to be present in the background of our life. And so even when life brings its fair share of good things, these are tainted by the hurt we choose to hang on to.

Formalising our marriage relationship helps keep it together. If we formalised our friendships, would that not have the same effect?

Finally, on the subject of forgiveness, let me finish by saying that we would be wise to heed Jesus' warning in Matthew 6:14-15 *"For if you forgive men when they sin against you, your heavenly Father will also forgive you. But if you do not forgive men their sins, your Father will not forgive your sins."*

There is an argument for saying that to forgive someone, especially someone we are close to, can be one of the hardest things we can be asked to do in our day-to-day Christian walk. This is undoubtedly true, but is all part of 'walking the narrow road' that Jesus says in Matthew 7:14 *"leads to life."*

Covenant also carries with it the ingredient of **RISK.** In one sense all relationships carry with them the element of risk. The risk of being disappointed and the risk of being hurt. However, if all we focussed on were the potential pitfalls of relationship then the chances are that we would never get close to anyone. Having said that, a covenant relationship, on the face of it, does involve a higher degree of risk than our other relationships because the covenant is made before God. In effect what we are saying to God is that we guarantee that this relationship is going to work come what may.

Covenant also requires **EFFORT.** A relationship of such depth obviously demands that time be spent on it. However, time is a precious commodity and one that is often in short supply. In no particular order of importance we have our work commitments, family commitments, commitments to our Church and of course we have to find time to spend with God, and if we are to fulfil these commitments with all integrity, how much time do we have left? That is why I doubt there has been a real understanding of covenant when I hear that someone has a large number of these types of relationships, because it is obvious that the parties involved are not really spending any time on building the relationship. So covenant requires physical effort. But it also requires emotional effort because sometimes it is just plain hard work keeping the relationship going when it hits difficulties.

A difficult ingredient to achieve, but a necessary one, is the ingredient of **TRANSPARENCY.** It is not possible to have a meaningful relationship of any intimacy unless there is the resolve to be open and honest with each other. Over the years I have heard lots of talk, especially within the confines of Church, of the need to be transparent, and rightly so. However, it has been my experience that often, although not always, when people say there is transparency within their relationships, this is not generally the case. The reason for this reluctance to be transparent is that in being so we make ourselves vulnerable.

We can only safely share our heart with someone when there is a high degree of **TRUST** which is another necessary ingredient of covenant.

It is most certainly true that we have to learn to trust each other, but we will only do so when we believe that the one we are in relationship with is committed to us. **COMMITMENT**, my final ingredient, is something most people aspire to, and will readily profess, without realising how difficult it can be to achieve over the long term.

Loyalty, a willingness to forgive, risk, effort, transparency, trust and long-term commitment are all necessary ingredients of covenant and which, if you think about it, sum up what is required to enjoy a successful marriage. Different relationships, but governed by the same principles.

The Consequences of Covenant

It has saddened me to see people make a covenant together but then something happens to cause one of the parties to walk away from the other. Maybe there has been a disagreement between the two of them and the relationship falls apart. Jesus says this in Luke 17:1 :

> Then He said to the disciples, "It is impossible that no offences should come." (New King James Version)

What Jesus is saying is that it is impossible to go through life without at some time or other being offended by something or someone, and more likely than not it will be someone. In other words, what we are being told here is that we cannot avoid being offended; there is almost an inevitability about it and this is especially true in the case of close, long-term relationships. It is impossible to walk with someone for any length of time without at some time falling out with each other. Therefore, the challenge is to resolve the problem in such a way as to prevent the relationship being shipwrecked. My marriage is in a healthy state today because my wife and I have determined that relational disputes are not grounds to end it. It should be exactly the same with our other covenant relationships.

Maybe one of the parties does not fall out with their covenant partner, but falls out instead with the Church and finds somewhere else to worship. As a consequence their relationship just fades away. While in theory moving Church should not necessarily harm a relationship, in practice it is almost unavoidable, as being part of two different Church families will severely restrict the opportunities of fellowshipping together. What must also be taken into consideration is the actual reason for one of the parties leaving the Church in the first place. If they leave with a bad attitude, this will obviously have a detrimental effect on the covenant relationship because the bad attitude will be directed at their covenant partner's spiritual family. In the natural, how can our friendship with someone be unaffected if they have an unresolved problem with either our parents or our children? As it is in the natural, so it is in the spiritual.

Maybe something gets in the way of the relationship like, for example, one of the parties moving away from the area, maybe to take another job in a different part of the country, or maybe to retire to a better climate. This is a situation I have witnessed time and time again and what is interesting is that, unlike relational disputes, this does not seem to be considered as breaking covenant. Why should it be? The relationship is still intact albeit now from a distance. However, it is the distance that is the effective covenant breaker. If I were to permanently move away from my wife, nobody would consider that to be an acceptable course of action. So why is it any different when we move away from our covenant brother or sister? In fact, if a husband were to walk out on his wife, we certainly would not expect God to continue to bless him. My contention is that if we break covenant with our friend, we also move out of the blessing of God.

I am aware that this interpretation of scripture has in the past been used to exert control over people, and where this has been the case this has obviously been wrong. However, an imbalance in application does not mean there is no truth in the principle. What I am **not** saying is that under no circumstances is it acceptable to leave a covenant partner. Even with marriage, scripture gives adultery as grounds for divorce, assuming of course that reconciliation has proved to be impossible. In the case of David and Jonathan, their relationship was effectively broken when David, his life under threat from Saul, was actually sent away by Jonathan.

1 Samuel 20:12-13

*Then Jonathan said to David: "By the LORD, the God of Israel, I will surely sound out my father by this time the day after tomorrow! If he is favourably disposed towards you, will I not send you word and let you know? But if my father is inclined to harm you, may the LORD deal with me, be it ever so severely, if I do not let you know and **send you away safely.**"*

In this situation David had no choice other than to leave Jonathan. If he had stayed then Saul would have had him killed. The key to this dilemma is the matter of choice. If we have no choice in the matter, then the breaking of covenant (not that David broke his covenant with Jonathan, it was more that the covenant was adversely affected) will not be upon our shoulders. What I am saying is that if we choose to move away from our covenant partners due to things like job opportunities and retirement issues, then what we are doing is putting more importance on these issues than on our covenant relationships, and it is this that is wrong and it is this that we will be held accountable for.

The following is a testimony which although not involving a covenant relationship situation, does cover the choice of either 'staying' or 'leaving' and is, I believe, therefore relevant. During the first half of 1991 I was placed in a situation of having to make a choice. At the time I was working in the finance industry as a branch manager of one of the UK's biggest building societies. I had been with them for thirteen years and moving from one branch to another, and therefore moving from one area of the country to another, had become a way of life, with each move generally meaning a bigger salary. But in 1991 I had a more important priority than money. I had become a Christian six years earlier while living and working in the East Yorkshire market town of Driffield and had then moved to Huddersfield in 1988. As a family we immediately began attending Huddersfield Christian Fellowship and had a real conviction that this was the Church where God wanted us to put down our roots. That conviction never left us and is still with us today. Three years after moving I was then faced with having to once again move, no doubt with a financial incentive to do so. My choice was quite straightforward; either stay in my job and leave the Church, or stay in the Church and leave my job. We really believed that God had brought us to Huddersfield and to cut a long story short, I decided that God had not changed His mind and so I left my job. Six months later I started working for the Church as the manager of its book shop before becoming part of the pastoral team two years later.

> ## Choosing material concerns over spiritual concerns is always unwise. The same is true when we put our material welfare above our duty to our covenant partners.

My point is that I made my spiritual concerns a higher priority than my material concerns. In working for the Church I took a 50% cut in salary and lost all my employment benefits - company car, final salary company pension, discounted mortgage interest rate etc - but all I wanted to do was what God wanted me to do. Twenty years later I can look back on two decades of blessing, not just for me, but for my family as a whole. Had I chosen to follow the material way, I am absolutely convinced that I would have missed out on what has turned out to be the most exciting and rewarding period of my life. Choosing material concerns over spiritual concerns is always going to be an unwise choice, and this is equally applicable to putting our material welfare above the duty we have to our covenant partners.

In the book of Ruth, even though the word 'covenant' is not actually used, we nevertheless see an outstanding example of someone valuing relationship over material security. In chapter one we see the Israelite Elimalech, his wife Naomi and their two sons relocate from Israel to Moab due to there being a famine in Israel. This must have been a difficult decision because of the animosity between the two kingdoms and it subsequently turns out to be a disastrous one as firstly Elimalech dies as do, some years later, both his sons. This leaves Naomi and her two Moabite daughters-in-law, Orpah and Ruth, (her sons having married while living in Moab) as widows. Naomi's decision to return to Israel now puts Orpah and Ruth in a difficult position. Do they stay in the land of their birth, or do they accompany their mother-in-law to face an insecure future in a country that would hardly be likely to embrace them? Ruth's response to the urging of Naomi for her to stay in Moab is a tremendous declaration of relational devotion.

Ruth 1:15-18

"Look," said Naomi, "your sister-in-law is going back to her people and her gods. Go back with her." But Ruth replied, "Don't urge me to leave you or to turn back from you. Where you go I will go, and where you stay I will stay. Your people will be my people and your God my God. Where you die I will die, and there I will be buried. May the LORD deal with me, be it ever so severely, if anything but death separates you and me." When Naomi realised that Ruth was determined to go with her, she stopped urging her.

On the face of it, Ruth was taking a huge gamble, and indeed on their arrival back in Israel she was reduced to having to forage for leftover grain in order to survive. However, her commitment to Naomi is quickly rewarded in spectacular fashion. Not only does she marry Boaz, a man of wealth and influence and therefore in the process secure Naomi's future, but of course what she also does is take her place in the genealogy of King David and therefore of Christ. A remarkable payback for a covenant commitment, but one that is altogether in line with God's promise to bless relational unity.

The Benefit of Covenant

Bearing in mind the serious nature of making covenant and the far-reaching consequences that will befall us if we break covenant, you may be forgiven for wondering if it is a step worth taking. However, the point is that covenant is supposed to guarantee that a relationship we treasure will stand the tests of time and adversity. This not only has the benefit of achieving for us relational fulfilment but it also brings to our life the blessing of God.

It is important to realise that the benefits of covenant far exceed what we as individuals receive. There is also a benefit to the Church. The Apostle Paul makes an interesting plea in 1 Corinthians 1:10:

> *I appeal to you, brothers, in the name of our Lord Jesus Christ, that all of you agree with one another so that there may be no divisions among you and that you may be perfectly united in mind and thought.*

On the face of it, what Paul is asking seems quite reasonable. Jesus himself said in Matthew 12:25 that *"Every kingdom divided against itself will be ruined, and every city or household divided against itself will not stand,"* and of course *God's household* (Ephesians 2:19) is what the Church is meant to be. So Paul's instruction for the Church to be united and not divided seems to be well founded. But is it a reasonable instruction? Is it achievable? Is it remotely possible that any Church, especially a Church of some size as the Church in Corinth was, could achieve the state of unity that Paul insists upon and which, in actual fact, is essential if the Church is to fulfil its purpose of establishing and extending the Kingdom of God?

Covenant on a limited scale can maintain unity on a wider scale.

When I think of Huddersfield Christian Fellowship with its congregation of all ages, a congregation made up of people from not only different social and economic backgrounds, but also different cultural backgrounds; could it ever be a reality that *all of you agree with one another so that there may be no divisions among you and that you may be perfectly united in mind and thought.*? The answer to that question is a resounding 'yes' because **covenant on a limited scale can maintain unity on a wider scale.** A somewhat simplistic example of this would be that if I have a covenant relationship with a brother in Church and then something happens to potentially cause me to leave Church (maybe I have been offended in some way by somebody else), then that gives me a problem because, if I do leave Church, that will have a detrimental effect on my relationship with my covenant brother. So what the existence of the covenant does is to force me to sort out my problem within the Church and not leave. While this may sound the obvious thing to do, it has been my experience that most people will, if at all possible, avoid confrontation and leave Church rather than stay and implement the Matthew 18:15 principle of *"If your brother sins against you, go and show him his fault, just between the two of you."* In this way the existence of my covenant results in the dispute, which could potentially lead to division, being dealt with, thereby maintaining unity which, in turn, results in God's blessing, not only on me, but also on the Church.

Finally, I am under no illusions as to the difficulties involved in maintaining good relationships with each other, especially over the long term. Often it is a matter of blood, sweat and tears. However, putting in the required effort is worth every drop of blood, every bead of sweat and every single tear because in amongst it all, and at the end of it all, there is the blessing of God. While it is undoubtedly true that covenant is only one element in the wider subject of relationships, it is nevertheless an important principle by which we can all benefit from the favour of God.